Summertime Tote   2

Sunny Set   6

Anchors Away   9

Pretty Pencil Case   11

Sunny Shoulder Bag   13

Colorful Carryall   16

Special Effects   18

Earth-Friendly Tote   20

For pattern inquiries, please visit: www.go-crafty.com

summertime tote

Yarn
RED HEART *Kids*, 5oz/141g skeins, each approx 290yd/265m (acrylic)
- 1 skein #2358 Light Purple (A)
- 1 skein #2650 Pistachio (B)
- 2 skeins #2680 Jade (C)

Hook
- Size J/10 (6mm) crochet hook *or any size to obtain correct gauge*

Notions
Yarn needle
Stitch markers or safety pins

Finished Measurements
Approx 9"/23cm wide x 13"/33cm high (excluding straps)

Gauge
Hexagon = 4"/10cm diameter from point to point
Remember to check gauge for best results!

How To Make A Gauge Swatch
With C, ch 5; join with sl st in first ch to form a ring.
Rounds 1–2 Work same as Rounds 1–2 of hexagon motif. Swatch should measure approx 4"/10cm diameter. Adjust hook size if necessary to obtain correct gauge.

TOTE
Note Tote has a lining. Throughout pattern, "Outer Bag" refers to the public side of the bag (which is constructed from hexagons and pentagons), and "Lining" refers to the sc lining.

Outer Bag

Hexagon (make 12 total)
With C, ch 5; join with sl st in first ch to form a ring.
Round 1 (right side) Ch 2 (counts as dc), 2 dc in ring, [ch 2, 3 dc in ring] 5 times; ch 2—18 dc and 6 ch-2 sps. Join with sl st in 2nd ch of beginning ch-2. Fasten off.
Note Use A for Round 2 of first 6 motifs, and B for Round 2 of remaining 6 motifs.
Round 2 With A or B and right side facing, join A or B with sl st in any ch-2 sp, ch 2 (counts as dc), (2 dc, ch 2, 3 dc) in same ch-2 sp as joining; *ch 1, (3 dc, ch 2, 3 dc) in next ch-2 sp; repeat from * 4 times more; ch 1—36 dc, 6 ch-2 sps and 6 ch-1 sps. Join. Fasten off.

Pentagon (make 12 total)
With C, ch 5; join with sl st in first ch to form a ring.
Round 1 Work same as Round 1 on hexagon.
Note Use A for Round 2 of first 6 motifs, and B for Round 2 of remaining 6 motifs.
Round 2 With right side facing, join A or B with sl st in any ch-2 sp, ch 2 (counts as dc), (2 dc, ch 2, 3 dc) in same ch-2 sp as joining; *ch 1, (3 dc, ch 2, 3 dc) in next ch-2 sp; repeat from * 3 times more; 3 dc in next ch-2 sp—33 dc, 5 ch-2 sps and 4 ch-1 sps. Join. Fasten off.

Outer Base
With A, ch 4; join with sl st in first ch to form a ring.
Round 1 Ch 1, 6 sc in ring—6 sc. Join with sl st in first sc.
Round 2 Ch 1, 2 sc in first sc and in each sc around—12 sc. Join.
Round 3 Ch 1, sc in same sc as joining, 2 sc in next sc; [sc in next sc, 2 sc in next sc] 5 times—18 sc. Join.
Round 4 Ch 1, sc in same sc as joining and in next sc, 2 sc in next sc; [sc in next 2 sc, 2 sc in next sc] 5 times—24 sc. Join.
Round 5 Ch 1, sc in same sc as joining and in next 2 sc, 2 sc in next sc; [sc in next 3 sc, 2 sc in next sc] 5 times—30 sc. Join.
Round 6 Ch 1, sc in same sc as joining and in next 3 sc, 2 sc in next sc; [sc in next 4 sc, 2 sc in next sc] 5 times—36 sc. Join.
Round 7 Ch 1, sc in same sc as joining and in next 4 sc, 2 sc in next sc; [sc in next 5 sc, 2 sc in next sc] 5 times—42 sc. Join.
Round 8 Ch 1, sc in same sc as joining and in next 5 sc, 2 sc in next sc; [sc in next 6 sc, 2 sc in next sc] 5 times—48 sc. Join.
Round 9 Ch 1, sc in same sc as joining and in next 6 sc, 2 sc in next sc; [sc in next 7 sc, 2 sc in next sc] 5 times—54 sc. Join.
Round 10 Ch 1, sc in same sc as joining and in next 7 sc, 2 sc in next sc; [sc in next 8 sc, 2 sc in next sc] 5 times—60 sc. Join.
Round 11 Ch 1, sc in same sc as joining and in next 8 sc, 2 sc in next sc; [sc in next 9 sc, 2 sc in next sc] 5 times—66 sc. Join. Fasten off.

summertime tote

OUTER BAG ASSEMBLY

With right sides facing, place 6 pentagons next to each other in a line, alternating colors, with straight long edge at bottom. Whipstitch motifs tog through back lps with A. Whipstitch first motif to last motif so that a ring of 6 motifs is made (bottom row made). Repeat for 6 pentagons to form top row. Join 2 rows of hexagons in same manner for center of the tote.

With right sides facing, whipstitch outer base and bottom edge of bottom row tog through back lps with A.

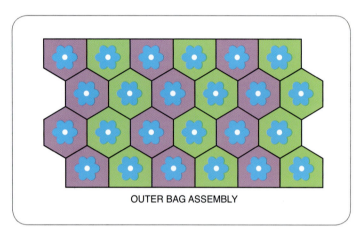
OUTER BAG ASSEMBLY

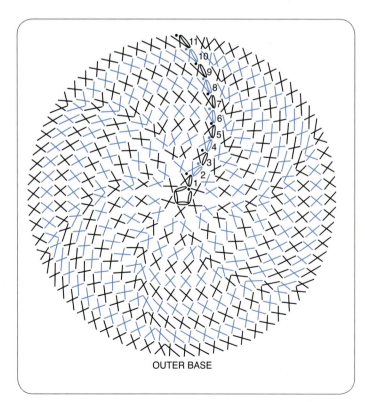
OUTER BASE

MOTIF RINGS ASSEMBLY

Taking care to line up points of one ring of hexagon motifs with valleys of bottom ring of pentagon motifs, whipstitch rings of motifs tog with right sides facing through back lps to create a flat bottom edge. Repeat with top ring of pentagon motifs and other ring of hexagon motifs to create a flat top edge. Join hexagon motif rings in center to form side of tote.

LINING Base and Sides

With C, ch 4; join with sl st in first ch to form a ring.

Rounds 1–11 Work same as Rounds 1–11 of outer base. At end of Round 11, do not fasten off.

Round 12 Ch 1, sc in same sc as joining and in each sc around—66 sc. Join.

Rounds 13–16 Repeat Round 12 four times more.

Round 17 Working in front lps only, repeat Round 12.

Rounds 18–26 Repeat Round 12 nine times more.

Round 27 Repeat Round 17.

Rounds 28–49 Repeat Round 12 twenty-two times more. At end of Round 49, fasten off.

Pen Pocket

With C, ch 16.

Row 1 (right side) Sc in 2nd ch from hook and in each rem ch across—15 sc. Ch 1, turn.

Rows 2–4 Sc in each sc across. Ch 1, turn. At end of Row 4, do not ch 1. Fasten off, leaving an 18"/45.5cm tail for sewing.

Square Pocket

With C, ch 21.

Row 1 (right side) Sc in 2nd ch from hook and in each rem ch across—20 sc. Ch 1, turn.

Rows 2–24 Sc in each sc across. Ch 1, turn. At end of Row 24, do not ch 1. Fasten off, leaving a 24"/61cm tail for sewing.

POCKET ASSEMBLY

Turn lining so wrong side is facing out. Line up bottom row of square pocket with some unused lps on Round 17 of lining. Line up one short edge of pen pocket with some unused lps on Round 27 of lining. Pin pockets in place with stitch markers. Using C, whipstitch bottom edge and 2 side edges of pockets to lining using unused lps on Rounds 17 and 27 of lining at bottom of pockets and sts running vertically up sides of lining from rounds with unused lps. Turn lining right side out with pockets on inside.

summertime tote

TOP EDGE OF BAG

Round 1 With right side of outer bag facing, join A with sc in any st on top edge of top ring of pentagon motifs, work 65 more sc evenly spaced around top edge (11 sc in top edge of each pentagon)—66 sc. Join with sl st in first sc. Fasten off.
Place lining inside outer bag with top edge of lining flush with top edge of outer bag. Pin in place with stitch markers.
Round 2 Working through both thicknesses of outer bag and lining, join C with sc in any sc of Round 1 and any sc on last round of lining, sc in each sc around. Join. Fasten off.
Round 3 With right side facing, join A with sc in any sc, sc in next 9 sc, 2 sc in next sc; [sc in next 10 sc, 2 sc in next sc] 5 times—72 sc. Join.
Round 4 Ch 2 (counts as dc), dc in next 6 sc, ch 2, sk next 2 sc; [dc in next 7 sc, ch 2, sk next 2 sc] 7 times—56 dc and 8 ch-2 sps. Join with sl st in 2nd ch of beginning ch-2.
Round 5 Ch 1, sc in same ch as joining, sc in each dc and in each ch around—72 sc. Join with sl st in first sc. Fasten off.
Round 6 With right side facing, join B with sc in any sc, working from left to right, work rev sc in each sc around—72 rev sc. Join. Fasten off.

STRAP

With B, ch 201.
Row 1 (right side) Sc in back bar of 2nd ch from hook in back bar of each rem ch across—200 sc. Fasten off.
Round 2 With right side facing, join A with sc in first sc, sc in each sc across, ch 1, pivot piece, sc in edge of last sc on Row 1, ch 1, pivot piece, working along opposite edge of foundation ch, sc in free lp of each ch across, ch 1, picot piece, sc in edge of first sc on Row 1, ch 1—402 sc. Join with sl st in first sc. Fasten off.

STRAP ASSEMBLY

Holding assembled bag upright, weave one end of strap in and out 4 consecutive ch-sps on Round 4 of top edge, starting and ending on right side, leaving approx 10"/25.5cm of opposite end of strap at beginning. Drop strap end down to bottom of bag. Insert strap end into a ch-sp on Round 1 at bottom straight long edge of bottom pentagon below 4th ch-sp where strap exited bag. Pushing strap between outer bag and lining, pull strap out another ch-sp on Round 1 at bottom straight long edge of next bottom pentagon approx 4"/10cm from where strap went in (below next available ch-sp on Round 4 of top edge). Bring strap end up to top of bag. Weave strap in and out next available ch-sp and following 3 consecutive ch-sps on Round 4 of top edge, starting and ending on right side. Tie two ends of strap tog in front. Adjust tension so that ends of strap are equal.

FINISHING

Weave in all ends. ■

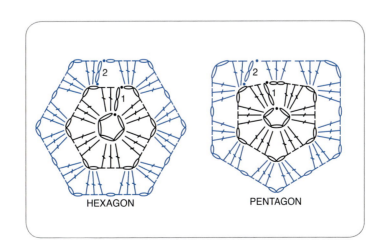

HEXAGON   PENTAGON

sunny set

Yarn
RED HEART *Soft Yarn*, 5oz/140g skeins, each approx 256yd/234m (acrylic)
- 2 balls #4420 Guacamole (A)
- 1 ball #4601 Off White (B)
- 1 ball #9537 Fuchsia (C)

Hook
Size H/8 (5mm) crochet hook *or any size to obtain correct gauge*

Notions
Yarn needle
2 buttons 1"/2.5cm diameter

Finished Measurements
Tote is approx 8"/20.5cm wide x 4½"/11.5cm deep (at base) x 8½"/21.5cm high
Sunglasses case is 3½"/9cm wide x 7½"/19cm long

Gauge
16 sc and 18 rows = 4"/10cm; 16 sc and 20 rounds = 4"/10cm using size H/8 (5mm) crochet hook.
Remember to check gauge for best results!

How To Make A Gauge Swatch
Ch 17.
Row 1 Sc in 2nd ch from hook and each ch across—16 sc.
Rows 2-18 Ch 1, turn, sc in each sc across.
Resulting gauge swatch should measure approx 4" x 4"/10cm x 10cm. Adjust hook size if necessary to obtain correct gauge.

STITCH GLOSSARY

2-dc Cl (2 dc cluster) Yo, insert hook in indicated sp, yo and draw up a loop, yo and draw through 2 loops on hook, yo, insert hook in same sp, yo and draw up a loop, yo and draw through 2 loops on hook, yo and draw through all 3 loops on hook.
3-dc Cl (3 dc cluster) Yo, insert hook in indicated sp, yo and draw up a loop, yo and draw through 2 loops on hook, [yo, insert hook in same sp, yo and draw up a loop, yo and draw through 2 loops on hook] twice, yo and draw through all 4 loops on hook.
sc2tog (sc 2 sts together) [Insert hook in next st, yo and draw up a loop] twice, yo and draw through all 3 loops on hook.

TOTE
Base
With A, ch 19.
Row 1 Sc in 2nd ch from hook and each ch across—18 sc.
Rows 2–36 Ch 1, turn. Sc in each sc across.
Fasten off.

Body
Join A with sl st in end of row at center of long edge of base.
Round 1 (right side) Sc in same row, sc in end of each row to corner (18 sc); ch 1, and pivot piece to work along sts of short edge, sc in each st across short edge (18 sc); ch 1, pivot piece to work along ends of rows of long edge, sc in end of each row to corner (36 sc); ch 1, pivot piece to work along short edge, sc in each st across short edge (18 sc); ch 1, pivot piece to work along beginning long edge, sc in each remaining sc across (18 sc); join with sl st in first sc—108 sc and 4 ch-1 sp.
Rounds 2–8 Ch 1, turn, *sc in each sc to next ch-1 sp, ch 1, sk ch-1 sp; repeat from * 3 more times, sc in each sc to end of round; join with sl st in first sc.
Fasten off A. Join B with sl st in first sc.
Rounds 9 and 10 Repeat Round 2 twice.
Fasten off B. Join A with sl st in first sc.
Round 11 (decrease round) Ch 1, turn, *sc in each sc across to last 3 sc before ch-1 sp, sc2tog, sc in next sc, ch 1, sk ch-1 sp, sc in next sc, sc2tog; repeat from * 3 more times, sc in each sc to end of round; join with sl st in first sc—100 sc and 4 ch-1 sp.

sunny set

Rounds 12–40 Repeat Rounds 2–11 twice, then repeat Rounds 2–10 once.
Fasten off B. Join A with sl st in first sc.
Rounds 41–43 Repeat Round 2 three times.
Fasten off A. Join B with sl st in first sc.
Round 44 (right side) Do not turn, working in back loops only, sl st in each sc around; join with sl st in first st. Fasten off.

STRAP
With A, ch 8.
Row 1 Hdc in 3rd ch from hook and each ch across—6 hdc.
Row 2 Ch 2, turn, hdc in each hdc across.
Repeat Row 2 until strap measures 18"/46.5cm. Fasten off.

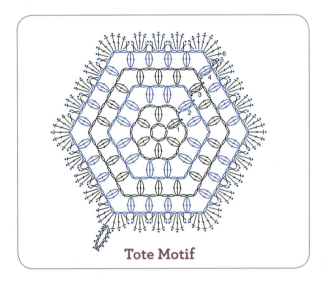

Tote Motif

MOTIF
With C, ch 6; join with sl st in first ch to form a ring.
Round 1 Ch 3, 2-dc Cl in ring, ch 4, *3-dc Cl in ring, ch 4; repeat from * 4 more times; join with sl st in top of beginning ch—6 ch-4 sp. Fasten off.
Round 2 Join A with sl st in any ch-4 sp, ch 3, (2-dc Cl, ch 4, 3-dc Cl) in same sp (corner made), ch 2, *(3-dc Cl, ch 4, 3-dc Cl) in next ch-4 sp (corner made), ch 2; repeat from * 4 more times; join with sl st in top of beginning ch. Fasten off.
Round 3 Join B with sl st in any ch-4 corner sp, ch 3, (2-dc Cl, ch 4, 3-dc Cl) in same sp, ch 2, 3-dc Cl in next ch-2 sp, ch 2, *(3-dc Cl, ch 4, 3-dc Cl) in next ch-4 sp, ch 2, 3-dc Cl in next ch-2 sp, ch 2; repeat from * 4 more times; join with sl st in top of beginning ch. Fasten off.
Round 4 Join A with sl st in any ch-4 corner sp, ch 3, (2-dc Cl, ch 4, 3-dc Cl) in same sp, ch 2, (3-dc Cl in next ch-2 sp, ch 2) twice, *(3-dc Cl, ch 4, 3-dc Cl) into next ch-4 sp, ch 2, (3-dc Cl in next ch-2 sp, ch 2) twice; repeat from * 4 more times; join with sl st in top of beginning ch. Fasten off.
Round 5 Join C with sl st in any ch-4 corner sp, ch 1, (sc, hdc, 5 dc, hdc, sc) in same sp, (sc, hdc, dc, hdc, sc) in next 3 ch-2 sp, *(sc, hdc, 5 dc, hdc, sc) in next ch-4 sp, (sc, hdc, dc, hdc, sc) in next 3 ch-2 sp; repeat from * once more, (sc, hdc, 3 dc) in next ch-4 sp, ch 10, sl st in top of last dc made (button loop made), (2 dc, hdc, sc) in same sp, (sc, hdc, dc, hdc, sc) in next 3 ch-2 sps,**(sc, hdc, 5 dc, hdc, sc) in next ch-4 sp, (sc, hdc, dc, hdc, sc) in next 3 ch-2 sp; repeat from ** once more; join with sl st in first sc. Fasten off.
Round 6 Working in back loops only, join B with sl st in any st, sl st in each st around; join with sl st in first st. Fasten off.

FINISHING
Sew ends of strap to short sides at top of tote.
Sew half of motif, with button loop to the front, to center top at back of tote.
Sew button to front of tote opposite button loop.
Weave in all ends.

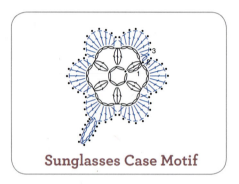

Sunglasses Case Motif

SUNGLASSES CASE
CASE
With B, ch 31.
Round 1 Sc in 2nd ch from hook and each ch across; taking care not to twist the sts, join with sl st in first sc to form ring—30 sc.
Round 2 Ch 1, turn, sc in each sc around; join with sl st in first sc.
Repeat Round 2 until case measures 7½"/19cm. Fasten off.

MOTIF
With C, ch 6; join with sl st in first ch to form a ring.
Round 1 Ch 3, 2-dc Cl in ring, ch 4, *3-dc Cl in ring, ch 4; repeat from * 4 more times; join with sl st in top of beginning ch—6 ch-4 sp. Fasten off.
Round 2 Join A with sl st in any ch-4 sp, ch 1, (sc, hdc, 5 dc, hdc, sc) in same sp and each of the next 2 ch-4 sps, (sc, hdc, 3 dc) in next ch-4 sp, ch 10, sl st in top of last dc made (button loop made), (2 dc, hdc, sc) in same sp, (sc, hdc, 5 dc, hdc, sc) in next 2 ch-4 sps; join with sl st in first ch. Fasten off.
Round 3 Working in back loops only, join B with sl st in any st, sl st in each st around; join with sl st in first st. Fasten off.

FINISHING
Seam bottom of case together using sl sts, then turn case inside out.
Sew half of motif, with button loop to the front, to center top at back of case.
Sew button to front of case opposite buttonhole.
Weave in all ends.

anchors away

Yarn
RED HEART *Sport*, 2.5oz/70g skeins, each approx 165yd/151m (acrylic)

- 2 skeins #853 Soft Navy (A)
- 2 skeins #316 Soft White (B)
- 1 skein #230 Yellow (C)

Hooks
Size I/9 (6mm) crochet hook *or any size to obtain correct gauge*
Size G/6 (4mm) crochet hook

Notions
Yarn needle
Stitch markers
Pins

Finished Measurements
Approx 14"/35.5cm wide x 14½"/37cm high plus handles

Gauge
12 sc and 13 rows = 4"/10cm using larger hook
Remember to check gauge for best results!

How To Make A Gauge Swatch
With 2 strands of yarn held together and larger hook, ch 13.
Row 1 Sc in 2nd ch from hook and in each rem ch across—12 sc.
Rows 2–13 Ch 1, turn; sc in each st across. Swatch should measure approx 4"/10cm square. Adjust hook size if necessary to obtain correct gauge.

STITCH GLOSSARY
Rev sc (reverse sc) Working from left to right, sc in next st to right of last st made.
Sc3tog (sc 3 stitches together) [Insert hook in next st, yo and draw up a lp] 3 times, yo and draw through all 4 lps on hook.

TOTE
Note Use larger hook and 2 strands of yarn held tog for tote.
With A, ch 41.
Round 1 (right side) Sc in 2nd ch from hook, sc in next ch and in each ch across to last ch, 3 sc in last ch, rotate work to work in free lps on other side of ch, sc in next 39 chs, 3 sc in skipped ch—84 sc. Place marker in first sc and move up to first sc in each round.
Round 2 Sc in each st around.
Rounds 3 and 4 Repeat Round 2 twice, changing to B in last sc of last round.
Rounds 5–8 With B, repeat Round 2, 4 more times, changing to A in last sc of last round.
Rounds 9–12 With A, repeat Round 2, 4 more times, changing to B in last sc of last round.
Rounds 13–48 Repeat Rounds 5–12, 4 more times, then repeat Rounds 5–8 once more. At end of last round, do not change to A. Join with sl st in first sc; fasten off.

Tote Edging
With right side facing, join C with sl st in any st on last round, work rev sc in each st around; join with sl st in first rev sc—84 rev sc. Fasten off.

anchors away

ANCHOR

Note Use smaller hook and 1 strand of yarn for anchor.

Anchor Top

With C, ch 6; join with sl st to form a ring.
Round 1 (right side) Ch 1, 12 sc in ring; join with sl st in first sc—12 sc. Fasten off.

Anchor Body

Round 1 (right side) Starting at top with C, ch 31, sc in 2nd ch from hook and in next 21 chs, ch 11, sc in 2nd ch from hook and in next 9 chs, sc in rem 8 chs of beginning ch-31; with right side of anchor top facing, sc in any sc on anchor top, 2 sc in next sc, [sc in next sc, 2 sc in next sc] 5 times; sc in free lps of first 8 chs of beginning ch-31, ch 11, sc in 2nd ch from hook and in next 9 chs, sc in free lp of next 22 chs of beginning ch-31, (sc, hdc, dc, hdc, sc) in skipped ch at beginning of ch-31. Join with sl st in first sc. Fasten off.

Anchor Bottom

With C, ch 46.
Round 1 (right side) Sc in 2nd ch from hook and in next 21 chs, 3 sc in next ch, sc in next 21 chs, 3 sc in last ch; rotate to work in free lps of chs, hdc in next ch, dc in next ch, (tr, ch 4, sl st) in next ch, sc in next 17 chs, sc3tog, sc in next 17 chs, ch 3, tr in next ch, dc in next ch, hdc in next ch, 2 sc in next ch; join with sl st in first sc. Fasten off.

BRAIDED HANDLES (make 2)

Note Use smaller hook and 1 strand of yarn throughout.

Strips (make 2 each with A, B and C)

With appropriate color, ch 91.
Row 1 (right side) Sc in 2nd ch from hook and in each rem ch across—90 sc. Fasten off.

Handle Bottom

Row 1 (right side) Using 3 strips, one of each color with right sides facing, join A with sl st in short end of first strip, ch 1, 2 sc in end of same strip, 2 sc in short end of next strip, 2 sc in short end of last strip—6 sc.
Rows 2–8 Ch 1, turn; sc in each sc across. At end of last row, fasten off.
Repeat handle bottom on other 3 strips.

Edging

With right side of handle bottom facing, join A with sl st in edge of first sc on Row 1, sc evenly around 3 sides of handle bottom, working 2 sc in each bottom corner; sl st in edge of last sc on Row 1. Fasten off.

Braid Strips

Secure handle bottom to a stationary object, such as seat of chair. With right side facing, braid strips, being careful not to twist strips. Secure at bottom of braid with a pin. Work handle bottom at pinned end of braid. Repeat for other braided handle.

FINISHING

With right sides facing, center and whip stitch anchor pieces to front of tote. Whipstitch handle bottoms to front and back of tote as shown in photograph. Weave in all ends.

pretty pencil case

Yarn
RED HEART *Soft*, 5oz/140g skeins, each approx 256yd/234m (acrylic)
- 1 skein #3720 Lavender (A)
- 1 skein #9623 Spearmint (B)

Hook
Size G/6 (4mm) crochet hook *or size to obtain gauge*

Notions
Yarn needle
Pins
Sewing needle and thread to match A
Zipper to match A or B—7"/18cm
Fabric lining—8¼x 9"/21 x 23cm (optional)
Peltex-Ultra stabilizer—7½x 8¼"/19 x 21cm (optional)

Finished Measurements
Case measures approx 9"/23cm long x 3"/7.5cm circumference.

Gauge
16 sc and 19 rows = 4"/10cm over single crochet
Remember to check gauge for best results!

How To Make A Gauge Swatch
Ch 17.
Row 1 Sc in 2nd ch from hook and in each rem ch across—16 sc.
Rows 2–19 Ch 1, turn, sc in each st across.
Resulting gauge swatch should measure approx 4 x 4"/10 x 10cm. If necessary, adjust hook size to obtain correct gauge.

Notes
1. The body of the pencil case is worked with the right side facing at all times.
2. You may fasten off the yarn at the end of each row. To reduce the number of ends to weave in, at the end of a row, carry the yarn back to the first stitch. As you work the next row with the second color, encase the loose strand under the single crochet stitches.
3. The body of the case is worked flat, then the stabilizer is applied. The ends are attached and a flower is sewn to each end.
4. Lining and stabilizer are optional, but they make the case sturdier.

BODY
With A, ch 36 loosely. (Note: The foundation chain should measure approx 8½"/21.5cm.)
Row 1 (right side) Sc in 2nd ch from hook, sc in each rem ch across—35 sc. Fasten off A (or carry A underneath B when working next row). Do not turn, work with right side facing throughout.
Row 2 Join B with sc in first sc of previous row, sc in each rem sc across. Fasten off B (or carry B underneath A when working next row). Do not turn.
Row 3 Join A with sc in first sc of previous row, sc in each rem sc across. Fasten off A (or carry A underneath B when working next row). Do not turn.
Rows 4–36 Repeat Rows 2 and 3, 16 times, then repeat Row 2 once more.
Piece should measure approx 7½x 8¾"/19 x 22cm. Block piece with steam iron, making sure sides are even.

END (make 2)
With B, ch 2.
Round 1 Work 10 sc in 2nd ch from hook; join with sl st in first sc—10 sc.
Round 2 Ch 1, 2 sc in each sc around; join with sl st in first sc—20 sc.
Round 3 Ch 1, 2 sc in first sc, sc in next sc, [2 sc in next sc, sc in next sc] 9 times; join with sl st in first sc—30 sc.
Round 4 Ch 1, sc in each sc around; join with sl st in first sc.
Round 5 Ch 1, 2 sc in first sc, sc in next 4 sc, [2 sc in next sc, sc in next 4 sc] 5 times; join with sl st in first sc—36 sc. Fasten off.

pretty pencil case

LARGE FLOWER (make 2)

With A, ch 2.

Round 1 Work 5 sc in 2nd ch from hook; join with sl st in first sc—5 sc.

Round 2 Ch 6, *sl st in next sc, ch 6; repeat from * around; join with sl st in first ch—5 ch-6 sps.

Round 3 *(Sl st, 6 sc) in next ch-6 sp, sl st in next sl st; repeat from * around; join with sl st in first sl st—5 petals. Fasten off.

SMALL FLOWER

With A, ch 2.

Round 1 Work 5 sc in 2nd ch from hook; join with sl st in first sc—5 sc.

Round 2 Ch 3, *sl st in next sc, ch 3; repeat from * around; join with sl st in first ch—5 ch-3 sps.

Round 3 *4 sc in next ch-3 sp, sl st in next sl st; repeat from * around; join with sl st in base of first sc—5 petals. Fasten off, leaving tail to attach to zipper pull.

FINISHING

Optional Facing and Lining

Cut stabilizer ¼"/6.5mm smaller than body on all sides. Cut fabric lining ½"/1.5cm larger than body on all sides. Center non-fusible side of stabilizer on wrong side of lining (fusible side showing). Fold edges of lining on top of fusible side of stabilizer and iron edges. Center wrong side of stabilizer (fusible side with edges overlapped) to wrong side of body. Tuck loose ends of yarn between body and stabilizer, and iron stabilizer to body with steam iron. With sewing needle and matching thread, sew loose edges of lining to body on all sides.

Assembly

Gently roll body into a tube. Pin end pieces to side edges of body, easing to fit.

Round 1 With body facing you, and end away from you, working through both thicknesses, join B with sc in any st, sc in each st around to join end to body; join with sl st in first sc. Fasten off. Join other end to opposite end of body in same manner. With sewing needle and matching thread, sew one flower to each end of case.

Set in Zipper

1. Keeping zipper closed, pin one side of zipper to top inside edge of case. With zipper closed, and using sewing needle and thread, hand stitch side of zipper to case edge. Make sure that loops of yarn are sewn down.

2. Unzip zipper and pin other side to opposite edge. Being careful to keep yarn away from the zipper closure, hand stitch this side while zipper is open. Stitch ends of zipper together, if needed. Sew small flower to zipper pull.

Weave in all ends. ■

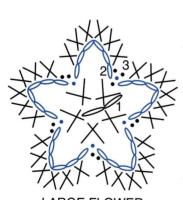
LARGE FLOWER

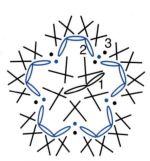
SMALL FLOWER

sunny shoulder bag

Yarn
RED HEART *Super Saver*, 7oz/198g skeins, each approx 364yd/333m (acrylic)
- 2 skeins #376 Burgundy (A)
- 1 skein #256 Carrot (B)
- 1 skein #321 Gold (C)
- 1 skein #905 Magenta (D)
- 1 skein #718 Shocking Pink (E)
- 1 skein #254 Pumpkin (F)

Hook
Size H/8 (5mm) crochet hook *or any size to obtain correct gauge*

Notions
Yarn needle
Cotton broadcloth fabric for lining (optional); 13½"/52cm x 33"/84cm
Sewing thread (optional)
Sewing needle or sewing machine (optional)

Finished Measurements
Approx 13½"/34.5cm wide x 14"/35.5cm high x 4½"/11.5cm deep

Gauge
motif = 4½"/11cm diameter from side to side (5"/13cm diameter from corner to corner)
Remember to check gauge for best results!

STITCH GLOSSARY

sc2tog (single crochet 2 stitches together) [Insert hook in next st, yarn over and draw up a loop] 2 times, yarn over and draw through all 3 loops on hook.

sc3tog (single crochet 3 stitches together) [Insert hook in next st, yarn over and draw up a loop] 3 times, yarn over and draw through all 4 loops on hook.

BAG
Motif (make 24)

Note
Use 3 or 4 colors to work hexagon motifs as desired. Colors are worked for 2 rounds before changing to a new color.
With first color, ch 2.

Round 1 (right side) Work 6 sc in 2nd ch from hook; join with sl st in first sc—6 sc.

Round 2 Ch 1, 2 sc in same sc as joining and in each sc around; join—12 sc. Fasten off.

Round 3 With right side facing, join 2nd color with sl st in first sc, ch 1, sc in same sc as joining, 3 sc in next sc, [sc in next sc, 3 sc in next sc] 5 times; join—24 sc.

Round 4 Ch 1, sc in same sc as joining and in each sc around; join. Fasten off.

Round 5 With right side facing, join 3rd color with sl st in first sc, ch 1, sc in same sc as joining and in next sc, 3 sc in next sc, [sc in next 3 sc, 3 sc in next sc] 5 times, sc in last sc; join—36 sc.

Round 6 Repeat Round 4.

Round 7 With right side facing, join 4th color with sl st in first sc, ch 1, sc in same sc as joining and in next 2 sc, 3 sc in next sc, [sc in next 5 sc, 3 sc in next sc] 5 times, sc in last 2 sc; join—48 sc.

Round 8 Repeat Round 4.

Round 9 With right side facing, join A with sl st in first sc, ch 1,

sunny shoulder bag

sc in same sc as joining and in next 3 sc, 3 sc in next sc, [sc in next 7 sc, 3 sc in next sc] 5 times, sc in last 3 sc; join—60 sc. Fasten off, leaving a long tail for joining.

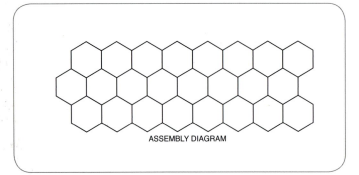

ASSEMBLY DIAGRAM

Motif Joining

With right sides facing, whipstitch back loops along edge of motifs tog with yarn needle and tail of A, starting and ending at center sc of 3 sc in corners. Join motifs into 3 rows with 8 motifs in each row, then join rows tog, staggering top and bottom of motifs as shown in diagram. Fold left and right edges of joined motifs tog and whipstitch back loops tog along edges to form a cylinder.

Top and Bottom "Valley" Fill-Ins

Row 1 With right side facing, join A with sl st in 2nd sc of 7 sc after 3 sc at top corner of any motif along top edge, ch 1, sc in same sc as joining and in next 6 sc, sc2tog in center sc of 3 sc in next corner of same motif and in center sc of 3 sc in adjacent corner of next motif, sc in next 7 sc on next motif, ending with sc in 6th sc of 7 sc before 3 sc at top corner of next motif—15 sc.
Row 2 Ch 1, turn; sc2tog, sc in next 4 sc, sc3tog, sc in next 4 sc, leaving last 2 sc unworked—10 sc.
Row 3 Ch 1, turn; sc2tog, sc in next sc, sc3tog, sc in next 2 sc, leaving last 2 sc unworked—5 sc. Fasten off.
Repeat Rows 1–3 until all 16 "valleys" have been filled in at top and bottom edges of bag.

Top Edge Border

Round 1 With right side facing, join A with sl st in center of 3 sc at tip of any motif along top edge of bag, ch 1, sc in same sc as joining, sc in each unworked sc on Round 9 of motifs, in each unworked sc on rows 1 and 2 of fill-ins and in each sc on Row 3 of fill-ins; join with sl st in first sc—112 sc.
Round 2 Ch 1, sc in same sc as joining and in each sc around; join. Fasten off.

Bottom Edge Border

Rounds 1 and 2 Work same as Rounds 1 and 2 of Top Edge Border along bottom edge of bag. Do not fasten off at end of Round 2.
Round 3 Repeat Round 2. Fasten off.

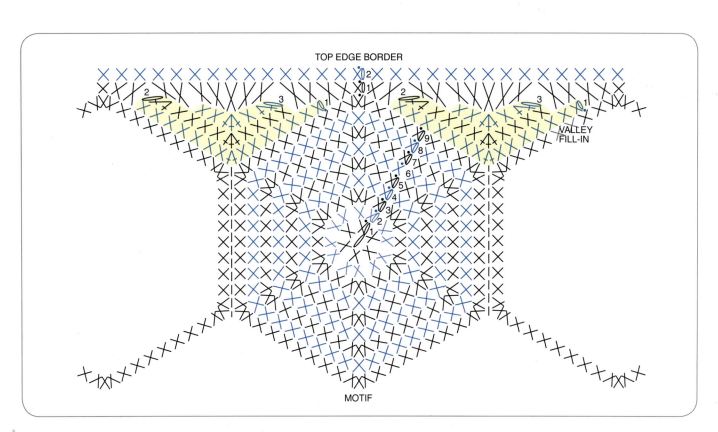

TOP EDGE BORDER
VALLEY FILL-IN
MOTIF

sunny shoulder bag

BOTTOM

With A, ch 42.

Row 1 (right side) Sc in 2nd ch from hook and in each remaining ch across—41 sc.

Rows 2–16 Ch 1, turn; sc in each sc across. At end of Row 16, fasten off.

Bottom Border

With right side facing, join A with sl st in first sc on row 16 of bottom, ch 1, sc in same sc as joining, sc in each sc across Row 16, sc in edge of each row, sc in free loop of each foundation ch across Row 1, sc in other edge of each row; join with sl st in first sc—114 sc. Fasten off.

Joining Bottom to Sides

With wrong sides tog, pin Bottom to Round 3 of Bottom Edge Border on bag, with long edges of Bottom lined up with 3 motifs for each side of bag and short edges of Bottom lined up with 1 motif for each end of bag. Working through both thicknesses, join A with sl st in back loop of any st, ch 1, sc in back loop of same st and in back loop of each st around, easing in fullness as needed. Fasten off.

STRAP

Row 1 With right side of Top Edge Border of bag facing, join A with sl st in sc on Round 2 of Top Edge Border directly above 6th sc before top corner of motif at either end of bag, sc in next 11 sc on Round 2 of Top Edge Border—12 sc.

Rows 2 and 3 Ch 1, turn; sc in each sc across.

Row 4 Ch 1, turn; sc2tog, sc in each sc across to last 2 sc, sc2tog—10 sc.

Rows 5 and 6 Repeat Row 2 twice.

Row 7 Repeat Row 4—8 sc.

Rows 8–133 Repeat Row 2, 126 more times until strap measures approx 36"/91.5cm, or to desired length.

Row 134 Ch 1, turn; 2 sc in first sc, sc in each sc across to last sc, 2 sc in last sc—10 sc.

Rows 135–136 Repeat Row 2 twice.

Row 137 Repeat Row 134—12 sc.

Rows 138–139 Repeat Row 2 twice. At end of last row, fasten off. Sew last row to Top Edge Border on opposite side of bag, centering above motif at other end of bag.

Strap Border

With right side facing, join A with sl st in first sc on Top Edge Border after either end of Strap, ch 1, sc in same sc as joining, sc in each sc across Top Edge Border to other end of Strap, sc in edge of each row on Strap; join with sl st in first sc. Fasten off. Repeat Border along other half of Top Edge Border and other edge of Strap.

FINISHING

Weave in ends.

Lining (optional)

Fold fabric in half lengthwise with right sides tog so piece is 16½"/42cm x 20½"/52cm. Sew 2 side seams. Turn down top edge 1"/2.5cm–1½"/4cm to wrong side and sew. Flatten bottom of lining a little and fold each bottom corner up approx 2½"/6.5cm toward side seam so that each corner looks like an envelope. Secure corner in place on side seam with a few stitches to form a flat bottom in lining. Do not turn lining. Insert lining inside bag, making sure that envelope folds are at ends of bag. Blind stitch top edge of lining to inside top edge of bag.

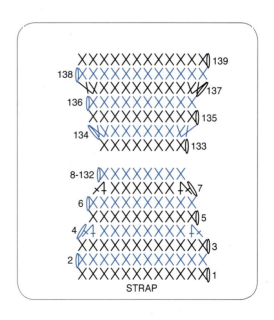

STRAP

colorful carryall

Yarn
RED HEART *Super Saver*, 7oz/198g skeins, each approx 364yd/333m (acrylic)
- 1 skein #319 Cherry Red (A)
- 1 skein #886 Blue (B)
- 1 skein #885 Delft Blue (C)
- 1 skein #512 Turqua (D)
- 1 skein #672 Spring Green (E)
- 1 skein #321 Gold (F)
- 1 skein #722 Pretty 'n Pink (G)
- 1 skein #774 Light Raspberry (H)

Hook
Size I/9 (5.5mm) crochet hook *or size to obtain gauge*

Notions
Yarn needle
Stitch markers
Two 5"/12.5cm high x 6½"/16.5cm-wide plastic horseshoe-shaped purse handles

Finished Measurements
Approx 17"/43cm wide at top x 13"/33cm high

Gauges
14 sc and 15 rows = 4"/10cm
Remember to check gauge for best results!

Note
Unless otherwise specified, each color is used for one round, then fastened off. Next color in sequence is used for following round. When all 8 colors have been used, start color sequence (A–H) over again.

TOTE

With A, ch 31.
Beginning Half Round Sl st in 2nd ch from hook (skipped ch counts as ch-1 sp) and in each rem ch across, ch 1—30 sl sts, and 2 ch-1 sps. Do not fasten off.
Round 1 (right side) Do not turn, pivot piece to work along opposite side of foundation ch, sc in each ch across; pivot piece to work in sts of Beginning Half Round, 3 sc in beginning ch-1 sp, sc in next 30 sl sts, 3 sc in next ch-1 sp—66 sc. Join with sl st in first sc. Fasten off.
Round 2 With right side facing, join B with sc in first st, sc in next 29 sts; *3 sc in next st (corner made), place a marker in first sc of corner just made, sc in next st, 3 sc in next st (corner made), place a marker in last sc of corner just made*; sc in next 30 sts; repeat from * to * once more—74 sc. Join. Fasten off.
Round 3 With right side facing, join C with sc in first st, [sc in each st to next marked st, 3 sc in marked st, move marker up to first sc of 3 sc just made, sc in each st to next marked st, 3 sc in marked st, move marker up to last sc of 3 sc just made] 2 times—82 sc. Join. Fasten off.
Rounds 4 and 5 Repeat Round 3 two more times, using D for Round 4 and E for Round 5. At end of Round 5—98 sc. Remove markers.
Round 6 With right side facing, join F with sc in any st, sc in each st around. Join. Fasten off.
Rounds 7–12 Repeat Round 6 six more times, using appropriate color in each round (Use G for Round 7 and H for Round 8. Start color sequence over again with A for Round 9).
Round 13 Flatten piece and place 2 stitch markers on front and back, approx 1½"/4cm from each side edge.
With right side facing, join E with sc in any st, [sc in each st to next marked st, 2 sc in marked st] 4 times; sc in each rem st—102 sc. Join. Fasten off. Remove markers.
Rounds 14–45 Repeat Rounds 6–13 four more times, using appropriate color in each round. At end of Round 45—118 sc.
Rounds 46 and 47 Repeat Round 6 two more times, using appropriate color in each round.
Round 48 With right side facing, join H with sc in any st, working from left to right, work rev sc in each st around—118 rev sc. Join with sl st in first sc. Fasten off.

TABS (make 4—optional)

With F, ch 8.
Row 1 Sc in back bar of 2nd ch from hook and in back bar of each rem ch across—7 sc. Fasten off, leaving an 8"/20.5cm tail for sewing.

JOINING HANDLES

Thread tabs through openings on ends of handles. Using yarn tails and yarn needle, sew ends of tabs in place on Round 46 on inside of tote. Optional: Instead of making tabs, stitch handles directly to tote.

FINISHING

Weave in all ends. ■

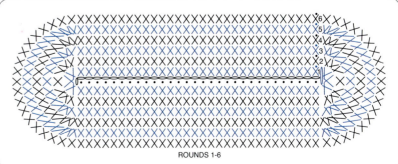

ROUNDS 1-6

special effects

Yarn
RED HEART *Super Saver*, 7oz/198g skeins, each approx 364yd/333m (acrylic)
- 1 skein #0313 Aran (A)
- 1 skein #0312 Black (B)

Hook
Size H/8 (5mm) crochet hook *or any size to obtain correct gauge*

Notions
Yarn needle

Finished Measurements
Approx 15"/38cm square plus 23"/58.5cm long handle

Gauge
Full Motif = 7"/18cm square
Motif Rows 1–4 = 2¾"/7cm square
Remember to check gauge for best results!

How To Make A Gauge Swatch
With A, ch 4, join with sl st to form a ring.
Rows 1–4 Work Rows 1–4 on Motif. Swatch should measure approx 2¾"/7cm square. Adjust hook size if necessary to obtain correct gauge.

Note
Motifs start at center and are worked in half rows.

STITCH GLOSSARY

sc2tog (sc 2 sts together) [Insert hook in next st, yo and draw up a lp] twice, yo and draw through all 3 lps on hook.

Row Join Drop lp from hook, insert hook in specified st and draw dropped lp through. To change colors: Work st until 2 lps rem on hook, drop old color, pick up new color, yo and draw through both lps on hook.

TOTE
Motif (make 8)

With A, ch 4; join with sl st to form a ring.
Row 1 (right side) Ch 3 (counts as dc now and throughout), 6 dc in ring—7 dc. Turn.
Row 2 Ch 3, 2 dc in first dc, dc in next 2 dc, 5 dc in next dc, dc in next 2 dc, 3 dc in 3rd ch of beginning ch-3 on Row 1—15 dc. Draw lp on hook out approx 2"/5cm, drop lp from hook.
Row 3 With right side facing, join B with sl st in ring to left of last dc made on Row 1; ch 3 (counts as dc), work row join in top edge of last dc on Row 1, 6 dc in ring, work row join in 3rd ch of beginning ch-3 on Row 1—7 dc. Turn.
Row 4 Ch 3, work row join in top edge of last dc on Row 2, 2 dc in first dc, dc in next 2 dc, 5 dc in next dc, dc in next 2 dc, 3 dc in beginning row join on Row 3, work row join in 3rd ch of beginning ch-3 on Row 2—15 dc. Do not turn.
Row 5 (wrong side) Working across Row 2 with B, ch 3, 2 dc in same ch as last row join, dc in next 6 dc, 5 dc in next dc, dc in next 6 dc, leaving lp at end of Row 2 hanging free, work 3 dc in last dc—23 dc. Turn.
Row 6 (right side) Ch 3, work 2 dc in first dc, dc in next 10 dc, 5 dc in next dc, dc in next 10 dc, 3 dc in 3rd ch of beginning ch-3 on Row 5—31 dc. Draw lp on hook out approx 2"/5cm, drop lp from hook.
Row 7 With wrong side facing, replace dropped lp of A from Row 2 on hook and working across Row 4, ch 3, work row join in top edge of last dc on Row 5, 2 dc in 3rd ch of beginning ch-3 on Row 4, dc in next 6 dc, 5 dc in next dc, dc in next 6 dc, 3 dc in last dc, work row join in 3rd ch of beginning ch-3 on Row 5—23 dc. Turn.
Row 8 Ch 3, work row join in top edge of last dc on Row 6, 2 dc in first dc, dc in next 10 dc, 5 dc in next dc, dc in next 10 dc, 3 dc in beginning row join on Row 7, work row join in 3rd ch of

special effects

beginning ch-3 on Row 6—31 dc. Do not turn.
Row 9 (right side) Working across Row 6 with A, ch 4 (counts as tr now and throughout), (tr, dc) in same ch as last row join, dc in next 14 dc, (dc, 3 tr, dc) in next dc, dc in next 14 dc, leaving lp at end of Row 6 hanging free, work (dc, 2 tr) in last dc—7 tr and 32 dc. Turn.
Row 10 Ch 4, (tr, dc) in first tr, dc in next 18 sts, (dc, 3 tr, dc) in next tr, dc in next 18 sts, (dc, 2 tr) in 4th ch of beginning ch-4 on Row 9—7 tr and 40 dc. Fasten off A.
Row 11 With right side facing, replace dropped lp of B from Row 6 on hook and working across Row 8, ch 4, work row join in top edge of last tr on Row 9, (tr, dc) in 3rd ch of beginning ch-3 on Row 8, dc in next 14 dc, (dc, 3 tr, dc) in next dc, dc in next 14 dc, (dc, 2 tr) in last dc, work row join in 4th ch of beginning ch-4 on Row 9—7 tr and 32 dc. Turn.
Row 12 Ch 4, work row join in top edge of last tr on Row 10, (tr,

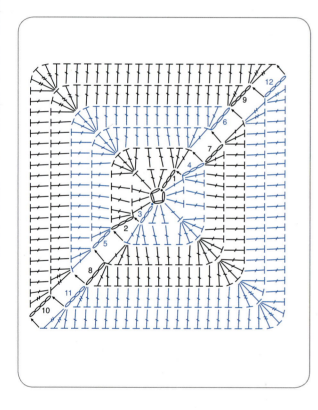

dc) in first tr, dc in next 18 sts, (dc, 3 tr, dc) in next tr, dc in next 18 sts, (dc, 2 tr) in beginning row join on Row 11, work row join in 4th ch of beginning ch-4 on Row 10—7 tr and 40 dc. Fasten off B.

ASSEMBLY

Front Panel

Arrange 4 motifs into a square with Row 10 of each motif in center of square. With wrong sides together, whipstitch motifs together through back lps only.

Back Panel

Arrange 4 motifs into a square with Row 12 of each motif in center of square. With wrong sides together, whipstitch motifs together through back lps only.

Panel Edging

With right side of Front Panel facing, join B with sl st in center tr of 3 tr in any corner, ch 1, sc in same st and in each st around 3 sides of panel, working 3 sc in each of 2 bottom corner sts (center tr of 3 tr in corner), ending with sc in center tr of 3 tr in last corner, leaving one edge unworked for top edge of panel. Sl st in same corner st. Fasten off.
Work Panel Edging on Back Panel with A in same manner.

Panel Joining

Hold Front and Back panels with right sides together, matching unworked top edge of each panel. Working in back lp only through both thicknesses, join B with sl st in first sc on panel edging, sl st in each sc around all 3 sides of panel edging. Fasten off. Turn right side out.

HANDLE

Foundation Row

With right side facing, join B with sl st in corner st at top right of Front Panel, working along top edge of Front Panel, ch 1, sc in same st as joining, sc in next 9 sts, sl st in next st and in each st across to last 10 sts on Front Panel, sc in last 10 sts, changing to A in last sc. Working along top edge of Back Panel with A, sc in first 10 sts, sl st in next st and in each st across to last 10 sts on Back Panel, sc in last 10 sts—2 groups of 20 sc each. Join with sl st in first sc. Fasten off.

First Half

Row 1 With right side facing, join B with sl st in first sc of either 20-sc group on foundation row, ch 1, sc in same sc as joining, sc2tog, sc in next sc and in each sc across to last 3 sc, sc2tog, sc in last sc—18 sc. Ch 1, turn.
Row 2 Sc in first sc and in each sc across. Ch 1, turn.
Row 3 Sc in first sc, sc2tog, sc in next sc and in each sc across to last 3 sc, sc2tog, sc in last sc—16 sc. Ch 1, turn.
Row 4–13 Repeat Rows 2 and 3 five times more—6 sc at end of Row 13.
Rows 14–45 Repeat Row 2 thirty-two times more, or until handle is half of desired length. Fasten off.

Second Half

Row 1 Repeat Row 1 on First Half of Handle, joining B with sl st in first sc of rem 20-sc group on foundation row.
Rows 2–45 Repeat Rows 2–45 on First Half of Handle. Whipstitch ends of handle halves together.

FINISHING

Weave in all ends.

earth-friendly tote

Yarn
RED HEART *Eco-Cotton Blend*, 3oz/85g skeins, each approx 145yd/132m (recycled cotton/acrylic)
• 6 skeins #1926 Currant

Hook
Size G/6 (4mm) crochet hook *or any size to obtain correct gauge*

Notions
Yarn needle
Stitch markers
Pins
9"/23cm circle of plastic canvas or heavy cardboard (optional)

Finished Measurements
Tote measures approx 28"/71cm circumference and 15½"/39.5cm tall (excluding strap).

Gauge
18 sts and 13 rows = 4"/10cm over half double crochet;
3 pattern repeats and 13 rows = 4"/10cm over body pattern stitch
Remember to check gauge for best results!

How to Make a Gauge Swatch
Ch 20.
Row 1 Sc in 2nd ch from hook and in each remaining ch across—19 sc.
Row 2 Ch 2, turn; hdc in first sc, *ch 3, sk next 2 sc, htr-pop in next sc, ch 3, sk next 2 sc, hdc in next sc; repeat from * across—3 htr-pop and 6 ch-3 sps.
Row 3 Ch 1, turn; sc in first hdc, *3 sc in next ch-3 sp, sk next htr-pop, 3 sc in next ch-3 sp, sc in next hdc; repeat from * across—22 sc.
Row 4 Ch 2, turn; dc in first sc, ch 3, sk next 3 sc, hdc in sp between last skipped sc and next sc, ch 3, sk next 3 sc, *htr-pop in next sc, ch 3, sk next 3 sc, hdc in sp between last skipped sc and next sc, ch 3, sk next 3 sc; repeat from * across, dc in last sc; repeat from * across—2 htr-pop, 6 ch-3 sps, and 1 dc at each end.
Row 5 Ch 1, turn, sc in first dc, 3 sc in next ch-3 sp, sc in next hdc, 3 sc in next ch-2 sp, *sk in next htr-pop, 3 sc in next ch-2 sp, sc in next hdc, 3 sc in next ch-2 sp; repeat from * across, sc in last dc—22 sc.
Row 6 Ch 2, turn, hdc in first sc, ch 3, sk next 3 sc, htr-pop in next sc, ch 3, sk next 3 sc, *hdc in sp between last skipped sc and next sc, ch 3, sk next 3 sc, htr-pop in next sc, ch 3, sk next 3 sc; repeat from * across, hdc in last sc.
Rows 7–10 Repeat Rows 3–6.
Rows 11–13 Repeat Rows 3–5.
Resulting gauge swatch should measure approx 4 x 4"/10 x 10cm. If necessary, adjust hook size to obtain correct gauge.

Notes
1. Body of bag is worked in rounds from the lower edge upward.
2. The bottom of the bag is worked separately and sewn to the lower edge of the body.
3. The strap is worked in two stages. First, lower sections of the strap are worked on both sides of the top of the bag. Then an insert is worked (for the top of the strap) and its edges sewn to the tops of the lower strap sections.

STITCH GLOSSARY
htr (half treble crochet) Yarn over twice, insert hook in indicated st, yarn over and draw up a loop (4 loops on hook), yarn over and draw through 2 loops on hook, yarn over and draw through all 3 loops on hook.
htr-pop (half treble crochet popcorn) 4 htr in indicated st, drop loop from hook, insert hook in first htr of group, insert hook back into dropped loop and draw through (popcorn completed).

BODY
Ch 120; being careful not to twist ch, join with sl st in first ch to form a ring.
Round 1 (right side) Ch 1, sc in same ch as join, sc in each remaining ch around; join with sl st in first sc—120 sts.
Rounds 2–6 Ch 2 (does not count as a st), beginning in same st as join, hdc in each st around; join with sl st in first hdc.
Round 7 Ch 5 (counts as hdc, ch 3), sk next 2 hdc, htr-pop in next hdc, ch 3, sk next 2 hdc, *hdc in next hdc, ch 3, sk next 2 hdc, htr-pop in next hdc, ch 3, sk next 2 hdc; repeat from * around; join with sl st in 2nd ch of beginning ch—20 pattern repeats (consisting of 20 htr-pop and 40 ch-3 sps).
Round 8 Ch 1, sc in same st as join, 3 sc in next ch-3 sp, sk next htr-pop, 3 sc in next ch-3 sp, *sc in next hdc, 3 sc in next ch-3 sp, sk next htr-pop, 3 sc in next ch-3 sp; repeat from * around; join with sl st in first sc—140 sc.

earth-friendly tote

Round 9 Ch 4 (counts as htr), 3 htr in first sc, drop loop from hook, insert hook in top of beginning ch, insert hook back into dropped loop, and draw through (beginning htr-pop completed), ch 3, sk next 3 sc, hdc in sp between last skipped sc and next sc (directly above htr-pop st below), ch 3, sk next 3 sc, *htr-pop in next sc (directly above hdc), ch 3, sk next 3 sc, hdc in sp between last skipped sc and next sc, ch 3, sk next 3 sc; repeat from * across; join with sl st in top of beginning htr-pop—20 htr-pop and 40 ch-3 sps.
Round 10 Ch 1, sc in beginning htr-pop, 3 sc in next ch-3 sp, sc in next hdc, 3 sc in next ch-3 sp, *sk next htr-pop, 3 sc in next ch-3 sp, sc in next hdc, 3 sc in next ch-3 sp; repeat from * around; join with sl st in first sc.
Round 11 Ch 5 (counts as hdc, ch 3), sk next 3 sc, htr-pop in next sc (directly above hdc), ch 3, sk next 3 sc, *hdc in sp between last skipped sc and next sc (directly above htr-pop), ch 3, sk next 3 sc, htr-pop in next sc, ch 3, sk next 3 sc; repeat from * around; join with sl st in 2nd ch of beginning ch.
Repeat Rounds 8–11 until body measures approximately 13½"/34.5cm from beginning, ending with an htr-pop row (Row 9 or Row 11).
Next Round Ch 1, 3 sc in each ch-3 sp around (do not sc into hdc or htr-pop sts); join with sl st in first sc—120 sts.
Next 4 Rounds Ch 1, hdc in each st around; join with sl st in first hdc.
Fasten off.

STRAP
Lower Strap Sections
With right side facing, decide which side you want as the front of the bag (front and back are open, with strap attached to sides). Flatten bag so that front is facing you. While bag is flat, count 17 sts from the side edge and place a marker in the next st. Flip bag over, so that back is facing you, and count 17 sts from the same side edge and place a marker in the next st. You will have 34 sts between markers. The first lower section of the strap is worked over these sts.
Row 1 Join yarn with sl st in sp between marked st and next hdc, hdc in next 34 sts, sl st in sp between st into which last hdc was worked and marked st; leave remaining sts unworked—34 hdc and 1 sl st on each end.
Row 2 Ch 1, turn; sk sl st, sk first hdc, hdc in each st to last hdc; leave last hdc and sl st unworked—32 hdc.
Rows 3–14 Ch 1, turn; sk first hdc, hdc in each st to last hdc; leave last hdc unworked—8 hdc.
Rows 15–21 Ch 1, turn; hdc in each hdc across.
Fasten off. Place markers on other side of bag as for first lower section of strap. Repeat Rows 1–21 on other side of bag.

Popcorn Insert for Top of Strap
Note This piece is worked separately and then sewn to the strap sides.
Ch 44.

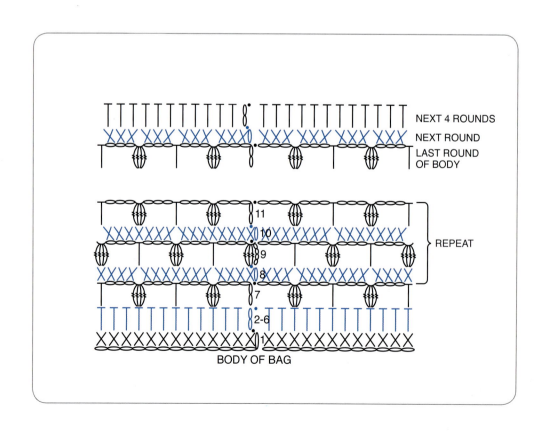

earth-friendly tote

Row 1 Sc in 2nd ch from hook and in each remaining ch across—43 sc.
Row 2 Ch 2, turn; hdc in first sc, *ch 3, sk next 2 sc, htr-pop in next sc, ch 3, sk next 2 sc, hdc in next sc; repeat from * across—7 htr-pop and 14 ch-3 sps.
Row 3 Ch 1, turn; sc in first hdc, *3 sc in next ch-3 sp, sk next htr-pop, 3 sc in next ch-3 sp, sc in next hdc; repeat from * across—50 sc.
Row 4 Ch 2, turn; dc in first sc, ch 3, sk next 3 sc, hdc in sp between last skipped sc and next sc, ch 3, sk next 3 sc, *htr-pop in next sc, ch 3, sk next 3 sc, hdc in sp between last skipped sc and next sc, ch 3, sk next 3 sc; repeat from * across, dc in last sc; repeat from * across—6 htr-pop, 14 ch-3 sps, and 1 dc at each end.
Row 5 Ch 1, turn; sc in first dc, 3 sc in each ch-3 sp across (do not sc into hdc or htr-pop sts), sc in last dc.
Fasten off. With right sides together and using yarn and yarn needle, sew ends of insert to tops of lower sections of straps.

Strap Edging

Join yarn with sc in any sc along top edge of bag, work sc evenly spaced around opening (including along edge of bag, one edge of strap and insert). Fasten off. Repeat around opposite opening.

BOTTOM

Ch 2.
Round 1 (right side) Work 9 hdc in 2nd ch from hook; join with sl st in first hdc—9 sts.
Round 2 Work 2 hdc in each hdc around; do not join—18 sts. Place a marker for beginning of round; move marker up as work progresses.
Round 3 [2 hdc in next hdc, place a marker in first hdc of 2-hdc group just made, hdc in next st] 9 times—27 sts (9 markers placed).
Rounds 4–15 [2 hdc in marked st, move marker to first hdc of 2-hdc group just made, hdc in each st to next marker] 9 times—135 sts.
Fasten off.

FINISHING

Turn body of bag inside out. With right sides of body and bottom together (wrong sides facing out), pin bottom to lower edge of body. With yarn and yarn needle, sew edges together, easing to fit. Turn bag right side out.

Weave in all ends. Place a circle (approx 9"/23cm) of plastic canvas or heavy cardboard inside bag bottom, if desired.

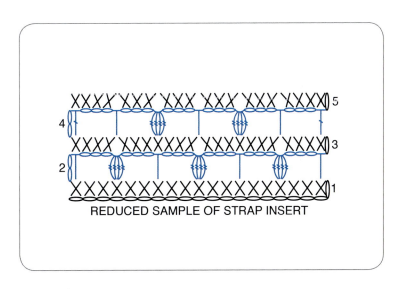

REDUCED SAMPLE OF STRAP INSERT

notes